Theo von Taane

AF171236

Baseball 2 in 1
Taktikboard & Trainingsbuch

Das 2 in 1 Taktikboard & Trainingsbuch zur schnellen Erstellung von coaching Anweisungen/Spieltaktiken und -plänen, enthält nicht nur sportspezifische Vorlagen (Spielfeld und Raum für Notizen), sondern verfügt auch über eine wieder beschreibbare Fläche (Cover des Buchs), welche mit handelsüblichen whiteboard Stiften beschrieben werden kann und trocken abwischbar ist.

VORTEILE:
- Taktikbuch mit sportspezifischen Vordrucken (Spielfeld) zum schnellen und einfachen Skizzieren von Spieltaktiken/Übungen.
- Sind alle Seiten des Buches aufgebraucht, lässt sich das Cover unter Nutzung von whiteboard Stiften als Taktikboard unbegrenzt weiternutzen.
- Durch das handliche Format sowohl unterwegs als auch vor Ort zum Spiel oder Training nutzbar.
- Ideal zum spontanen Sammeln von Trainingsideen oder als Gedankenstütze.
- Ideal um dem Spieler durch schnelles Skizzieren der Übung den geplanten Trainingsablauf begreifbarer zu machen.
- Ideal zum Festhalten von geplante Spielzügen, um sie sich kurz vor dem Match oder währenddessen wieder ins Gedächtnis zu rufen.

Bibliografische Information der Deutschen Nationalbibliothek:
Die Deutsche Nationalbibliothek verzeichnet diese Publikation in der Deutschen Nationalbibliografie; detaillierte bibliografische Daten sind im Internet über http://dnb.dnb.de abrufbar.

© 2016 Theo von Taane; 1. Auflage

Texte und Illustrationen: **Theo von Taane**

Herstellung und Verlag: BoD – Books on Demand, Norderstedt

ISBN: 9783739231327

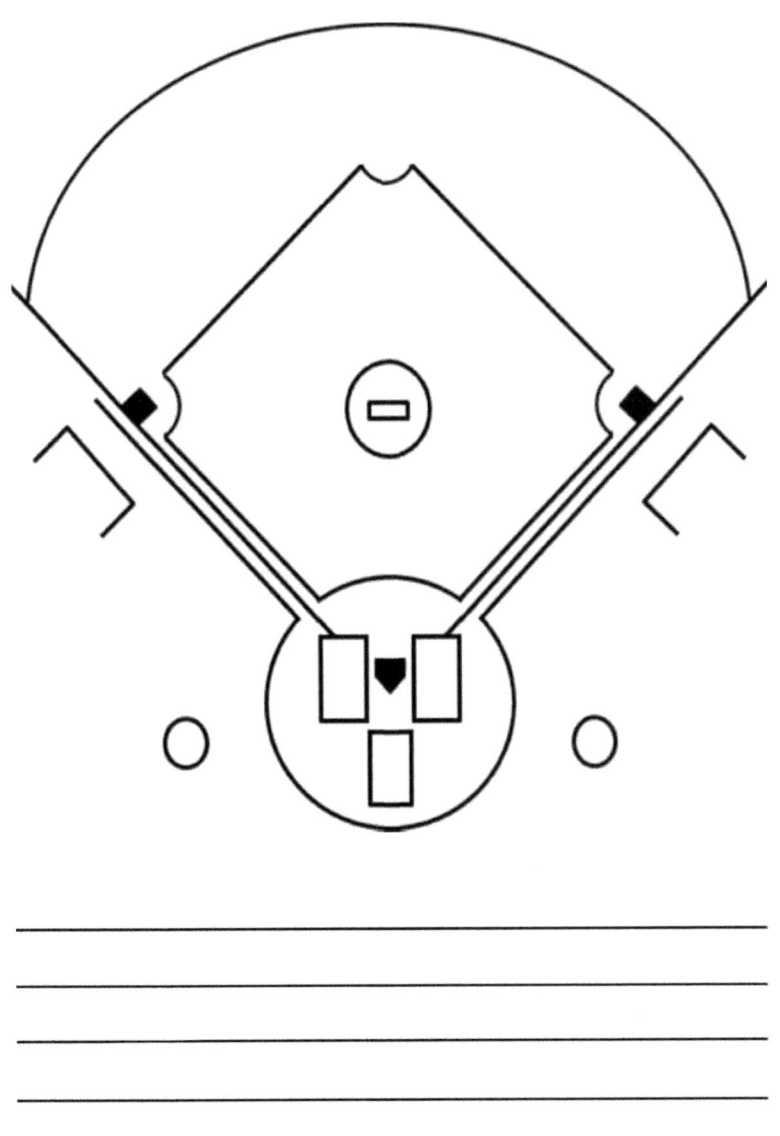

Inning of game	Player at bat	Batting position	Player number	Batter Lineup	Field position

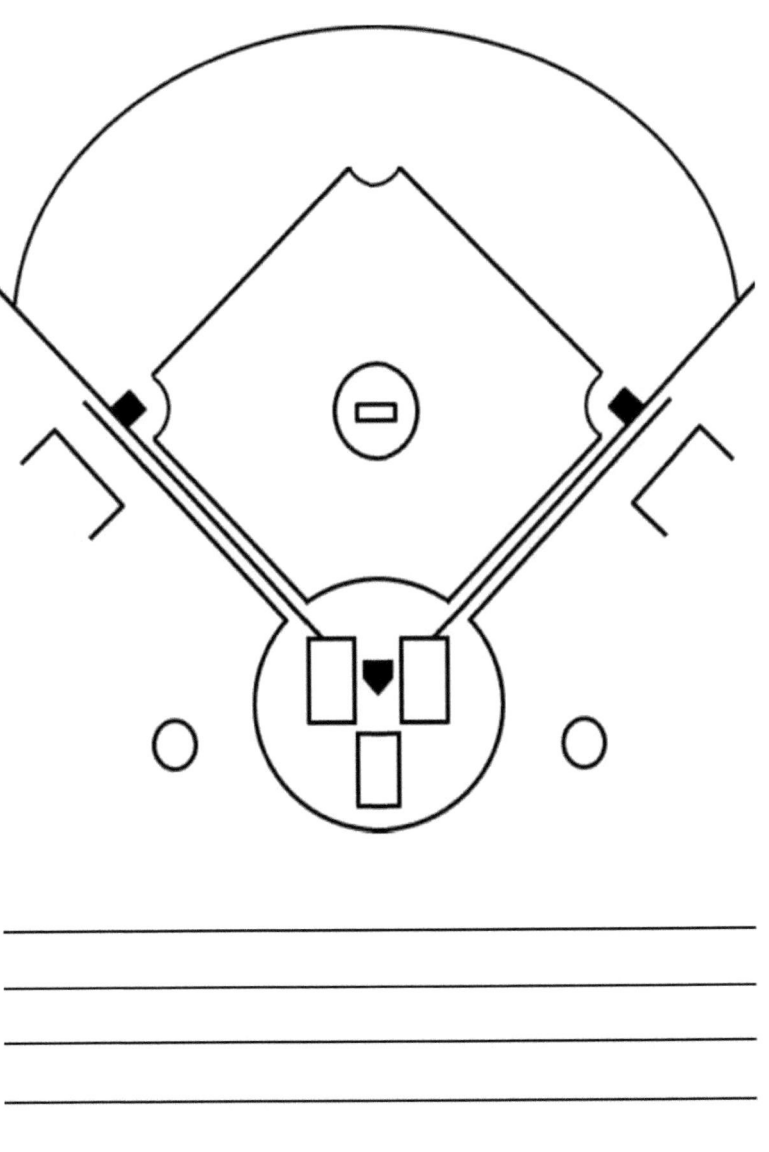

Inning of game	Player at bat	Batting position	Player number	Batter Lineup	Field position

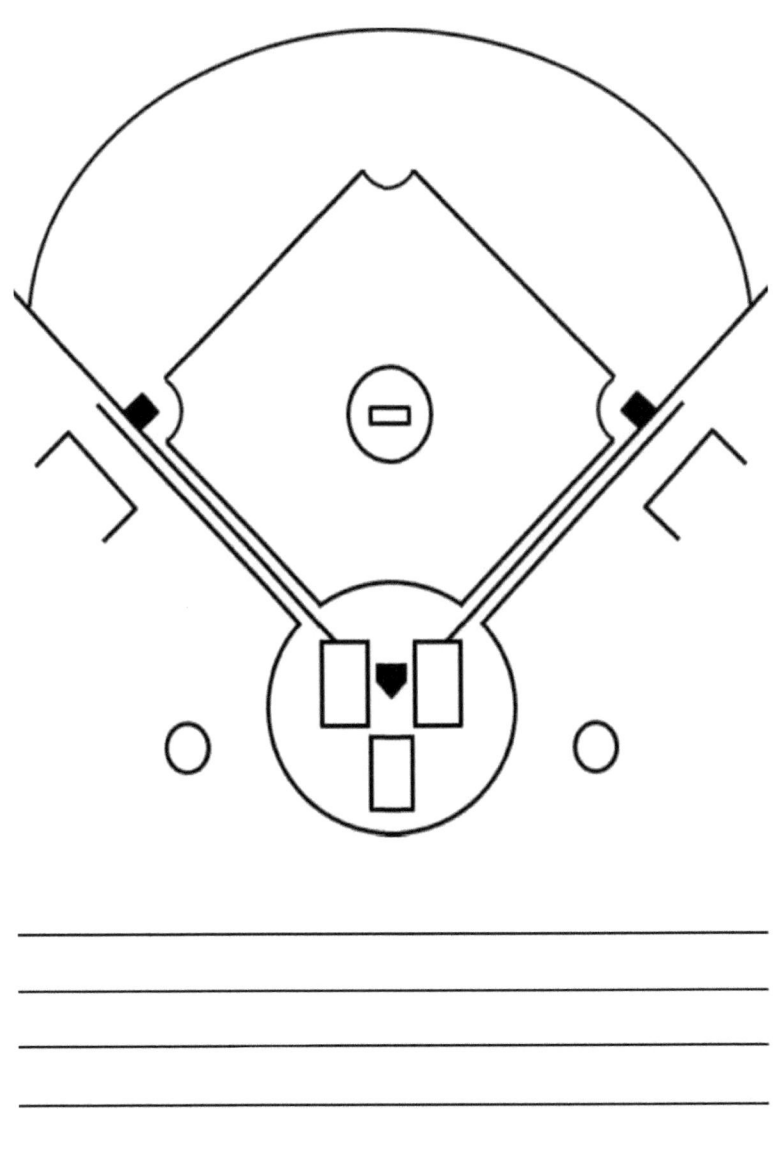

Inning of game	Player at bat	Batting position	Player number	Batter Lineup	Field position

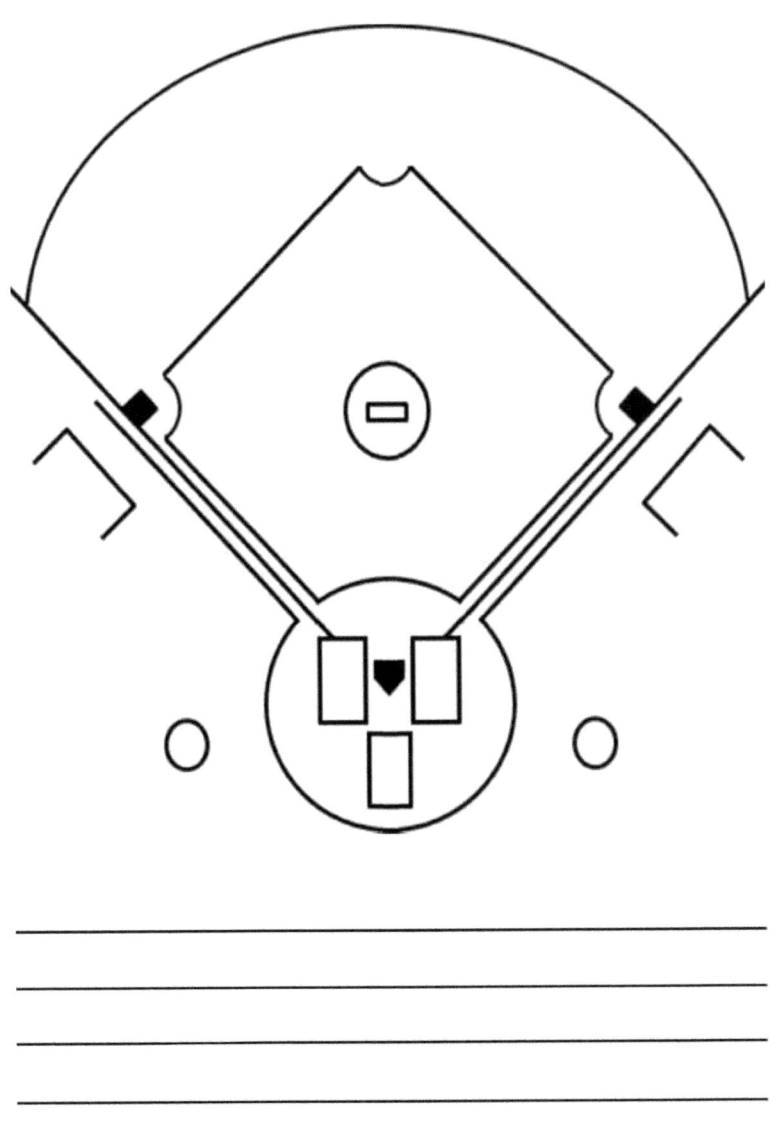

Inning of game	Player at bat	Batting position	Player number	Batter Lineup	Field position

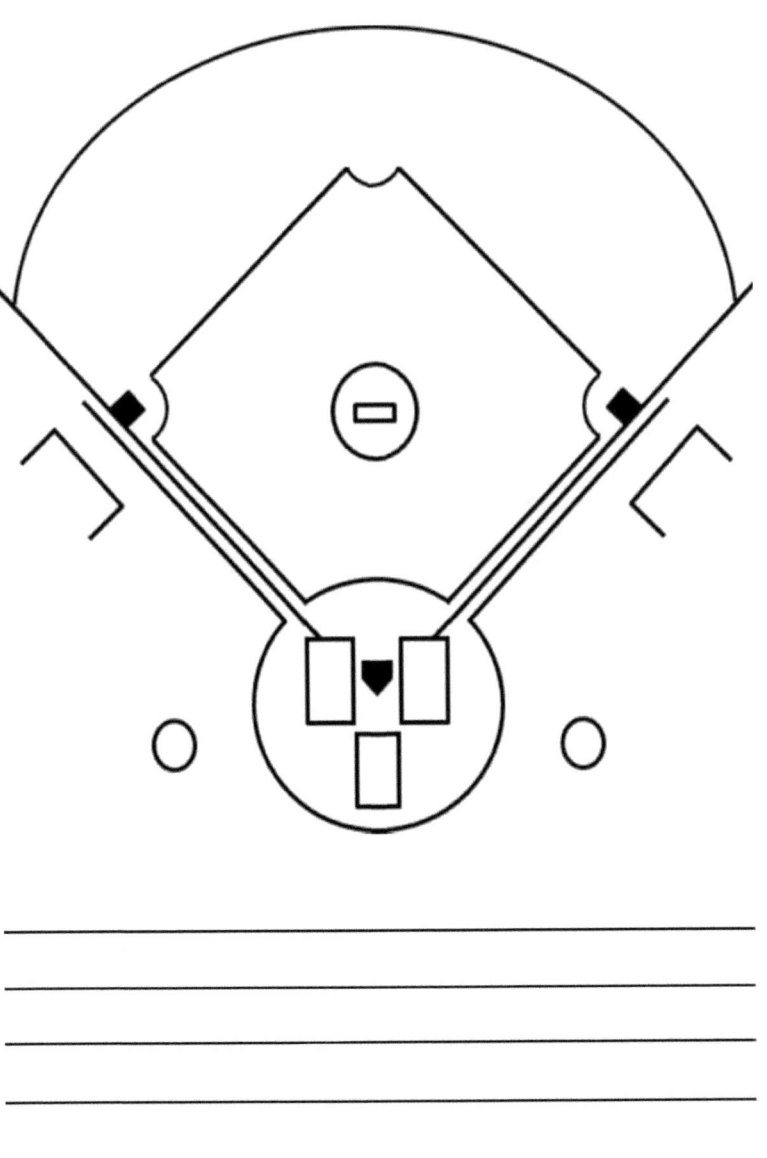

Inning of game	Player at bat	Batting position	Player number	Batter Lineup	Field position

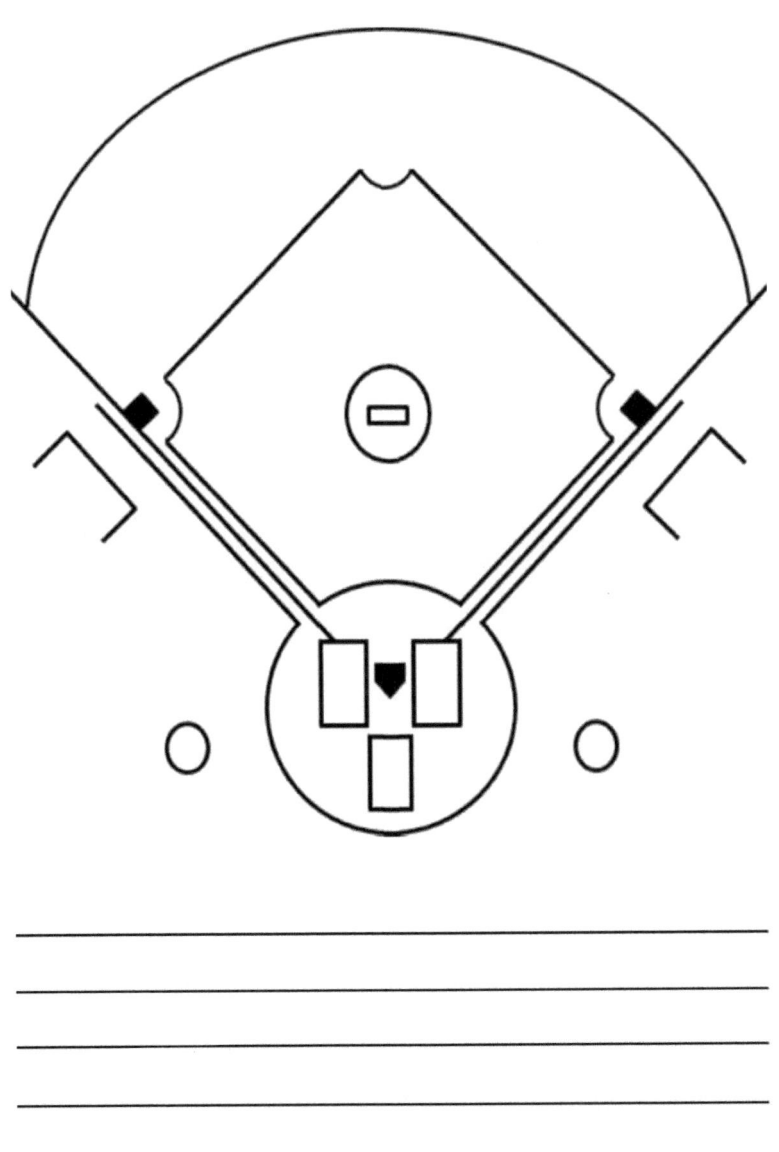

Inning of game	Player at bat	Batting position	Player number	Batter Lineup	Field position

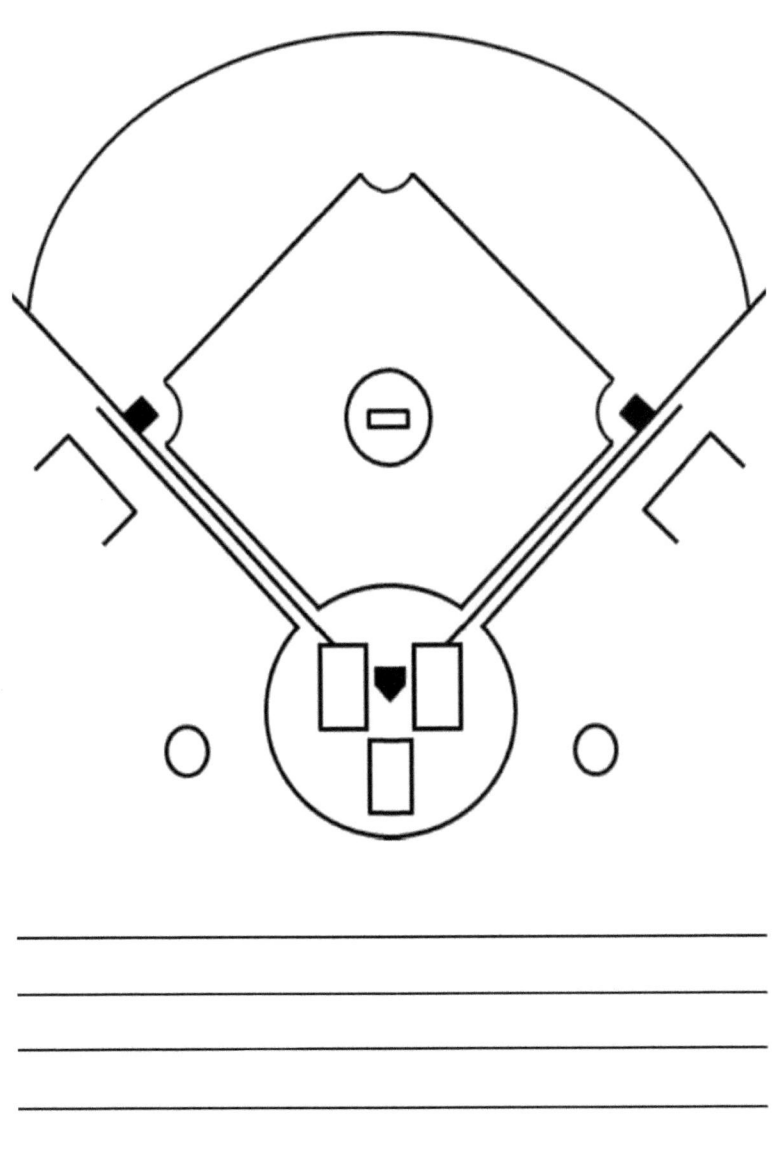

Inning of game	Player at bat	Batting position	Player number	Batter Lineup	Field position

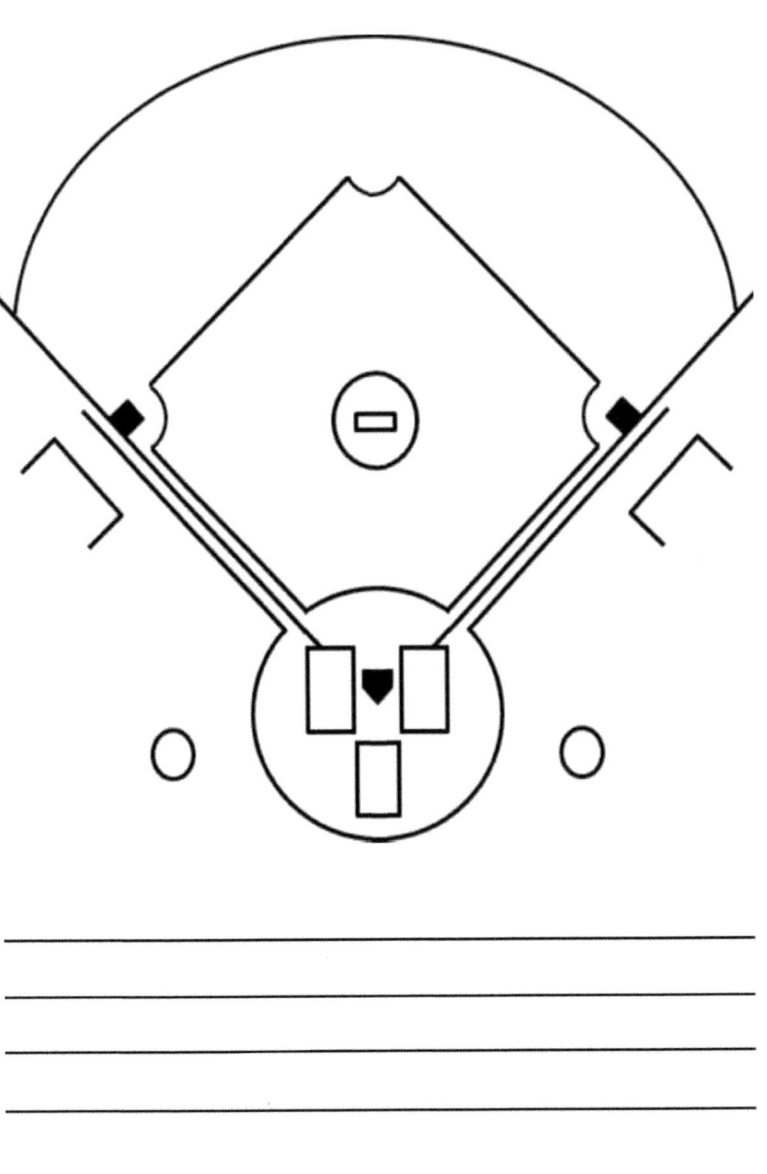

Inning of game	Player at bat	Batting position	Player number	Batter Lineup	Field position

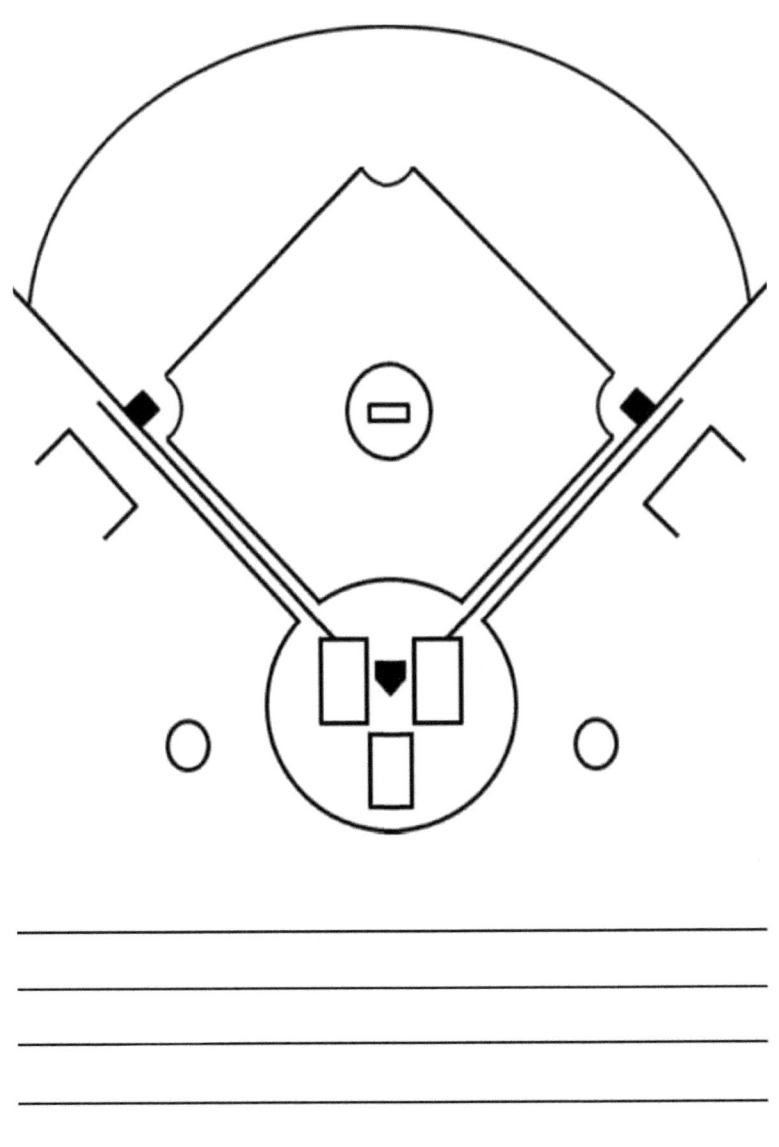

Inning of game	Player at bat	Batting position	Player number	Batter Lineup	Field position

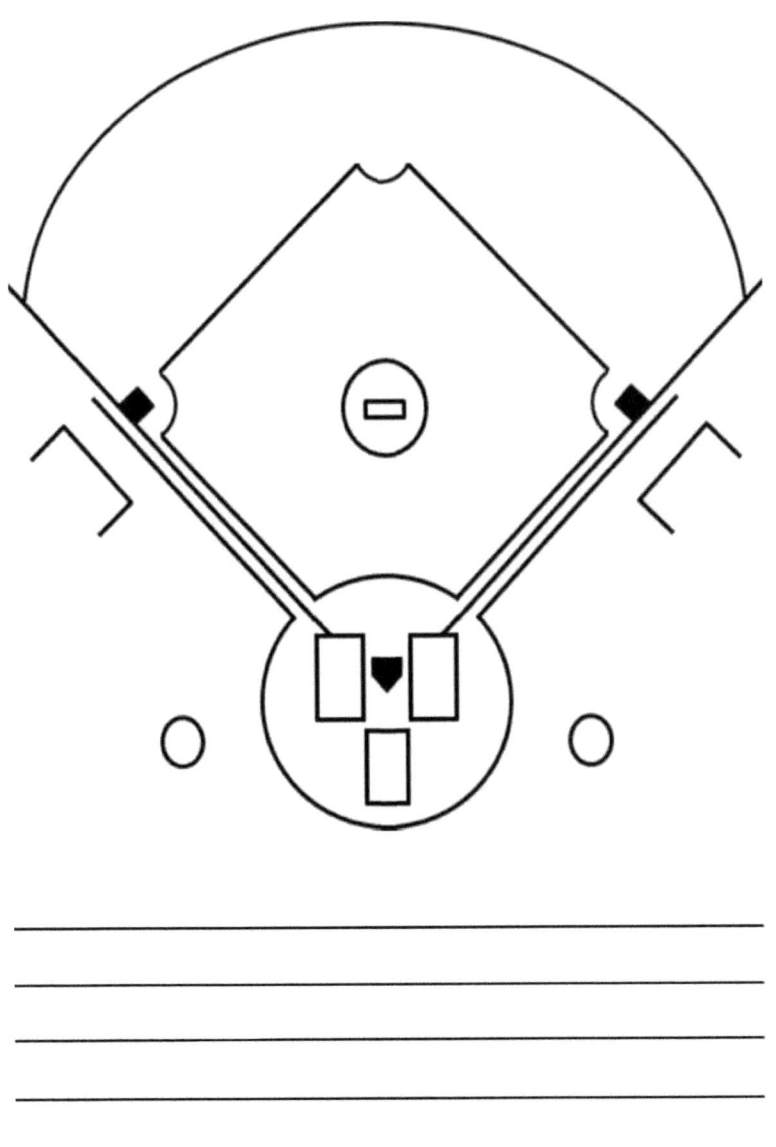

Inning of game	Player at bat	Batting position	Player number	Batter Lineup	Field position

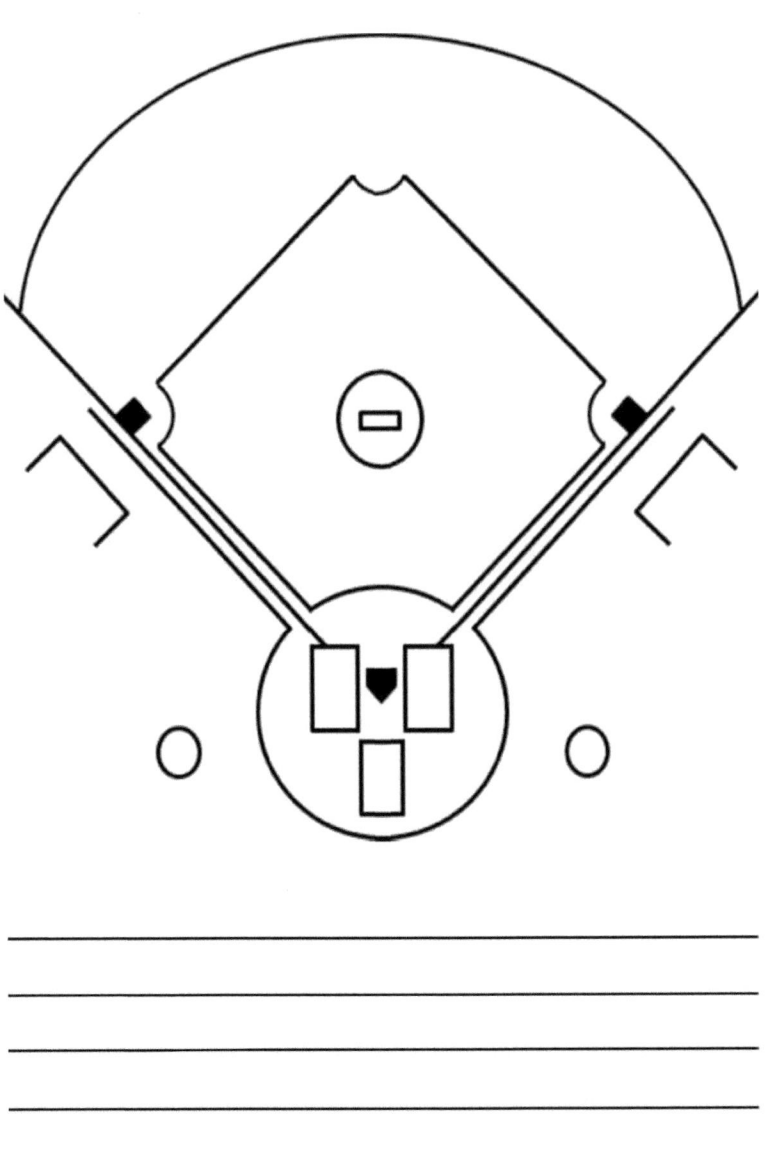

Inning of game	Player at bat	Batting position	Player number	Batter Lineup	Field position

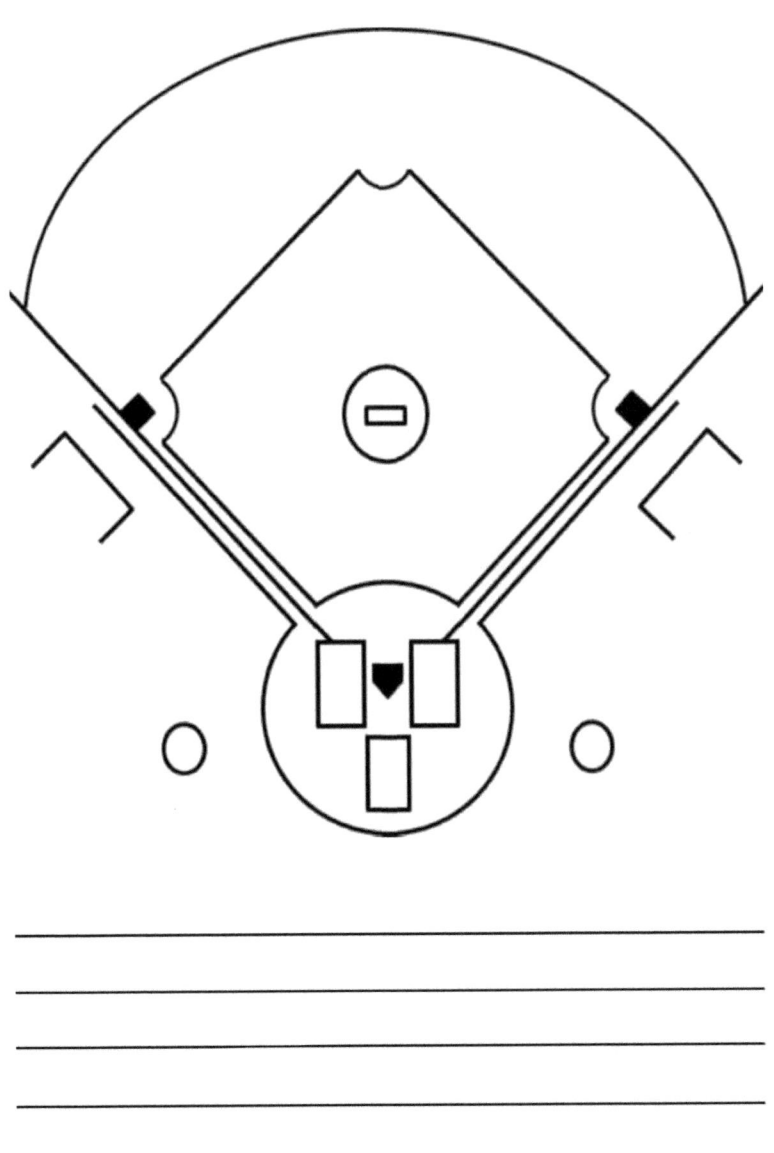

Inning of game	Player at bat	Batting position	Player number	Batter Lineup	Field position

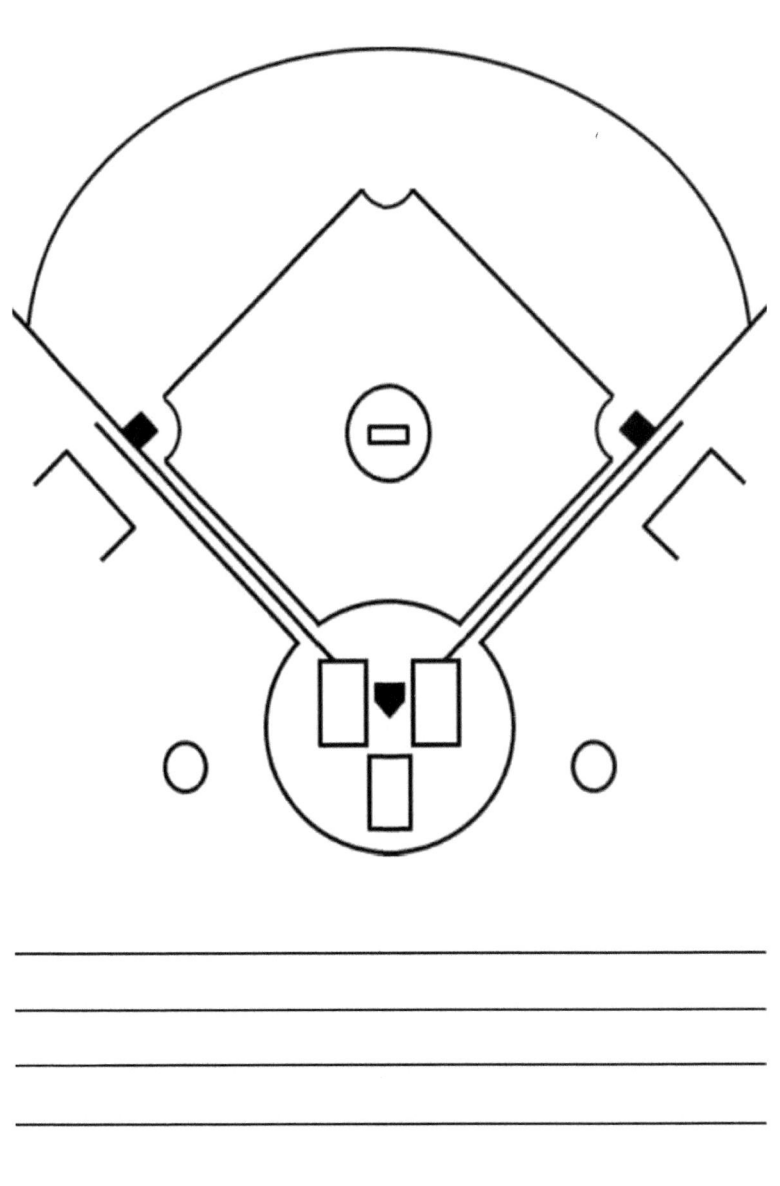

Inning of game	Player at bat	Batting position	Player number	Batter Lineup	Field position

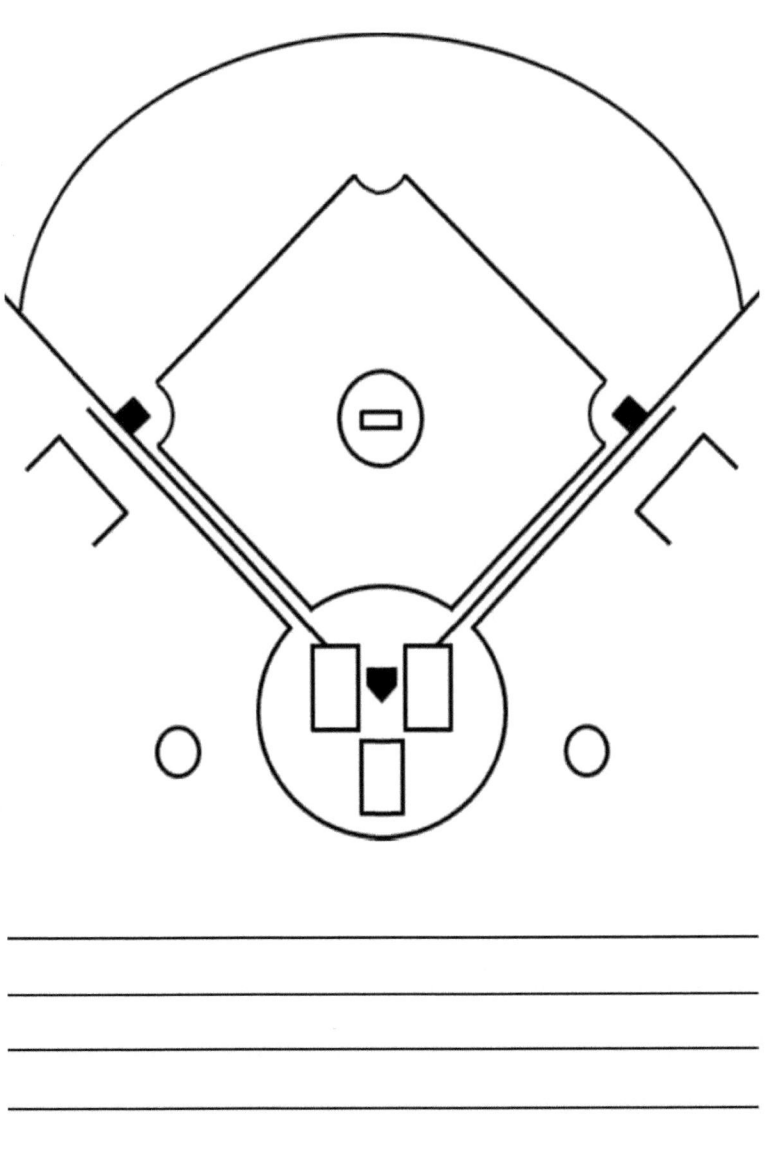

Inning of game	Player at bat	Batting position	Player number	Batter Lineup	Field position

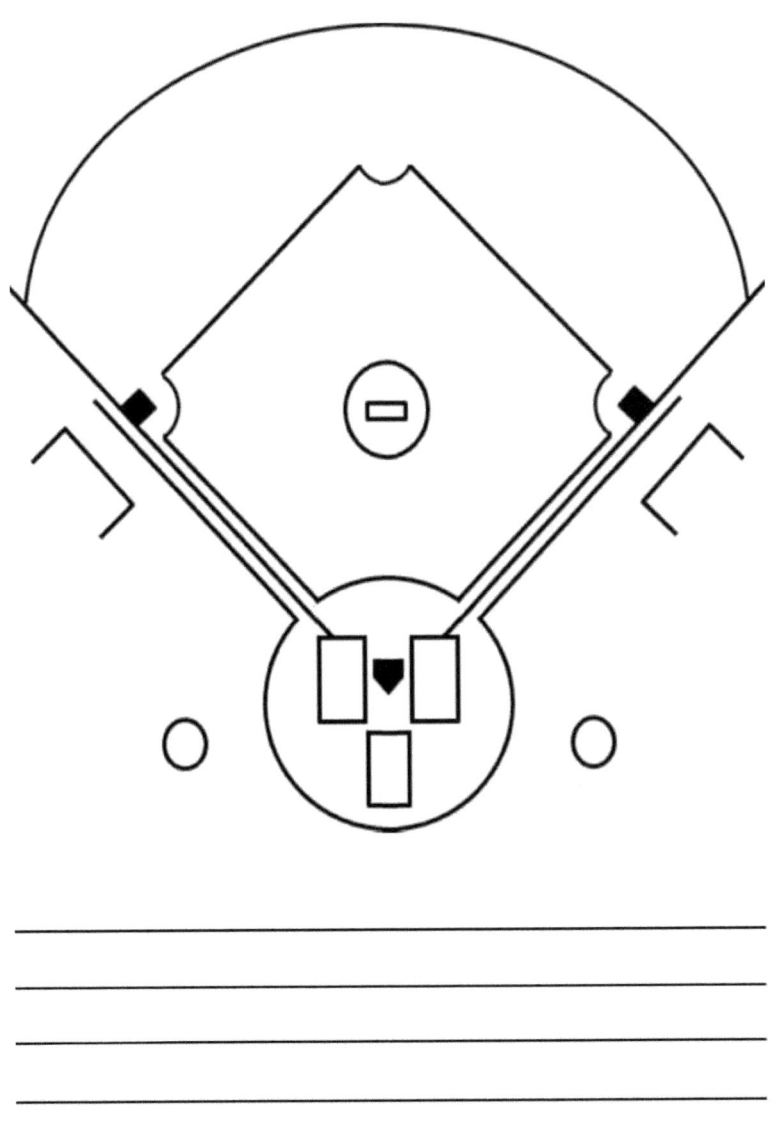

Inning of game	Player at bat	Batting position	Player number	Batter Lineup	Field position

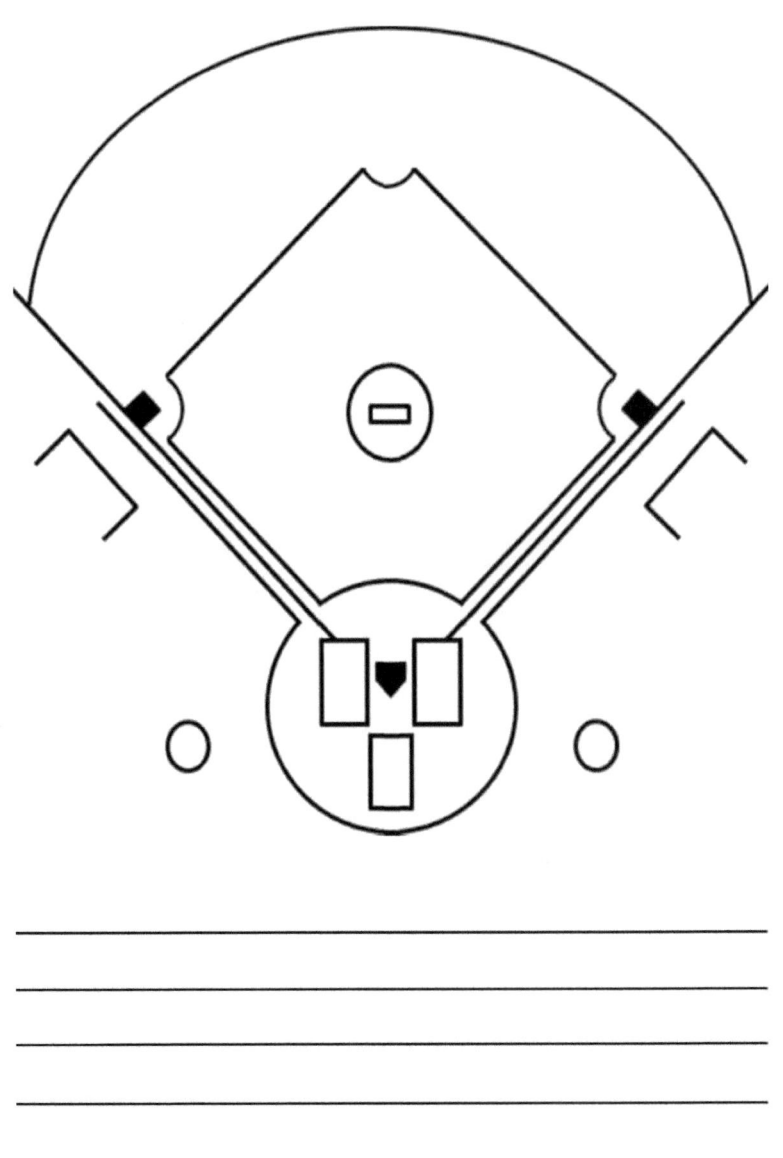

Inning of game	Player at bat	Batting position	Player number	Batter Lineup	Field position

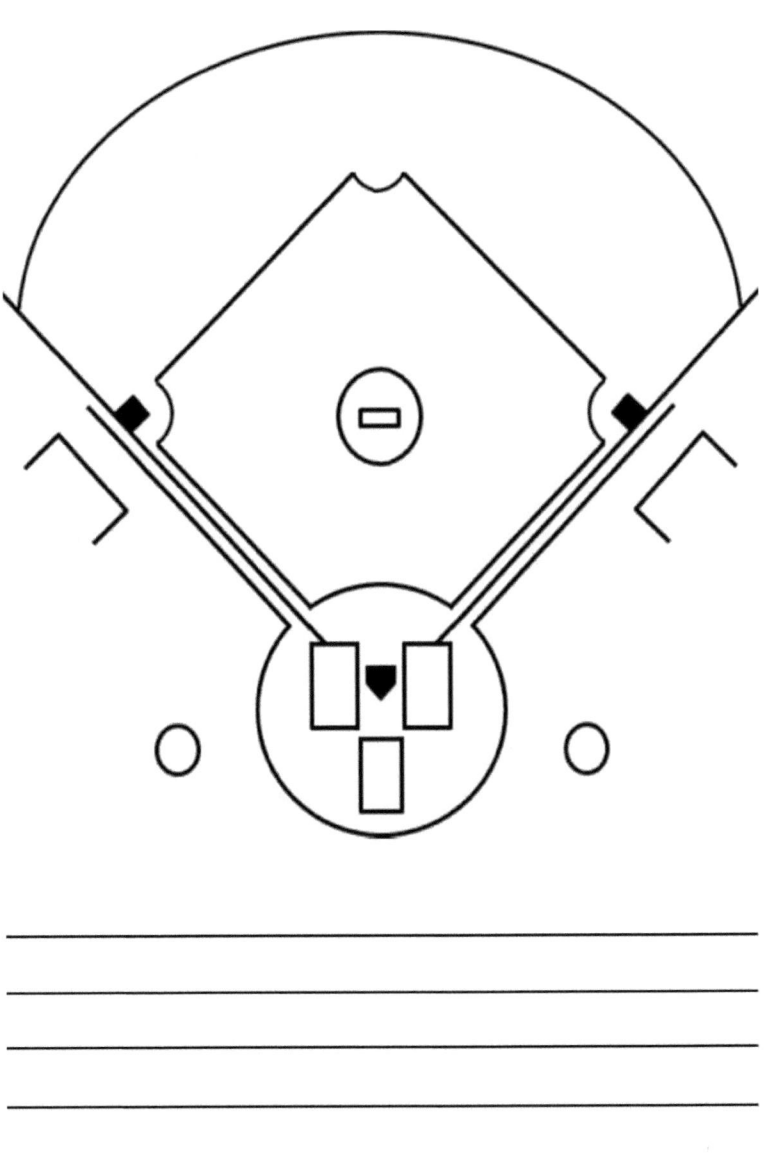

Inning of game	Player at bat	Batting position	Player number	Batter Lineup	Field position

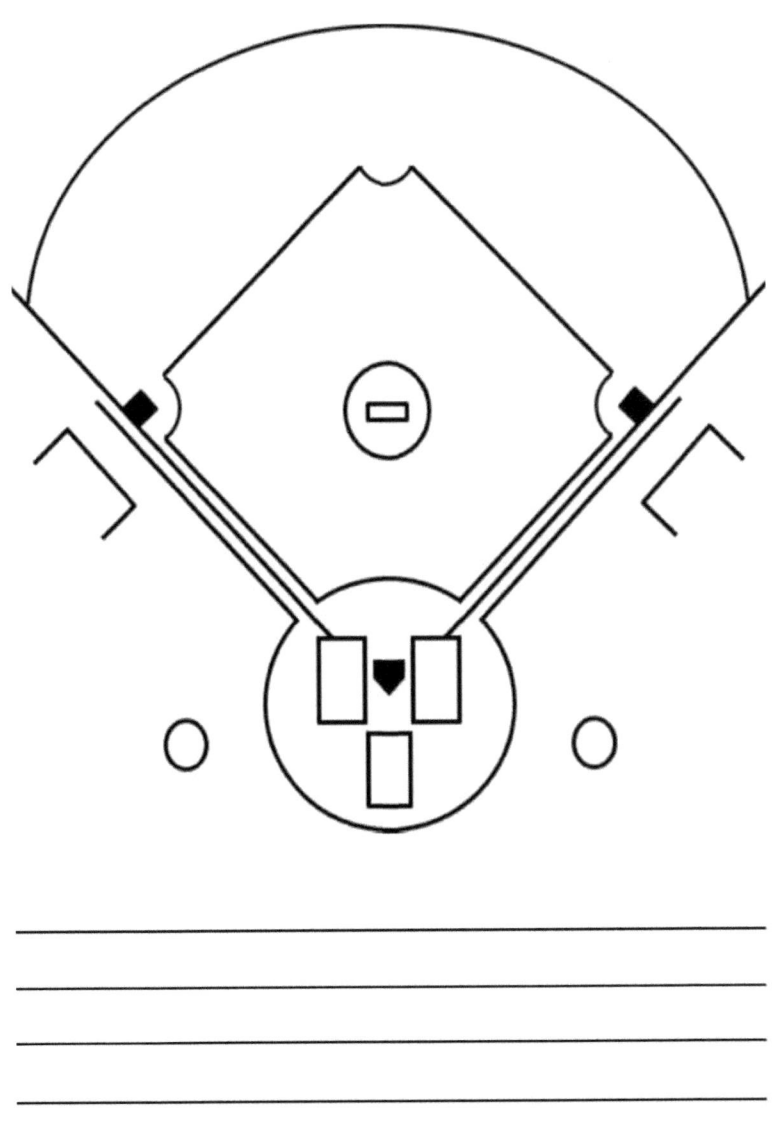

Inning of game	Player at bat	Batting position	Player number	Batter Lineup	Field position

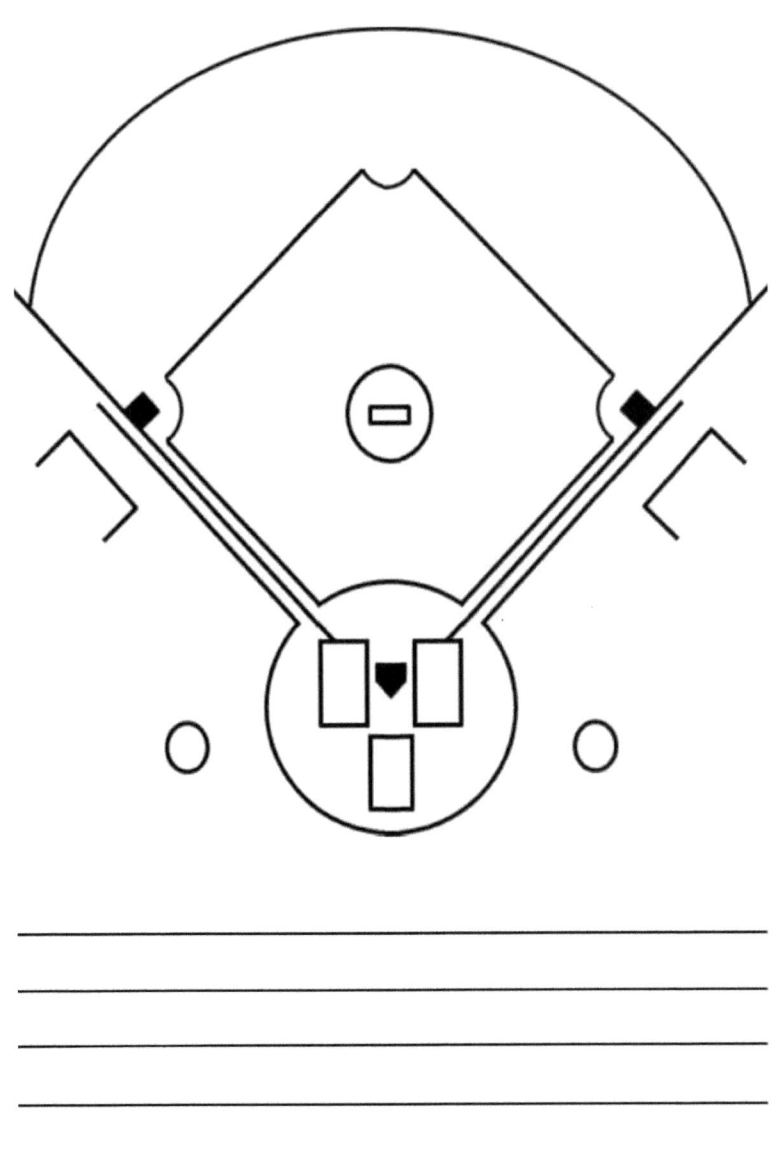

Inning of game	Player at bat	Batting position	Player number	Batter Lineup	Field position

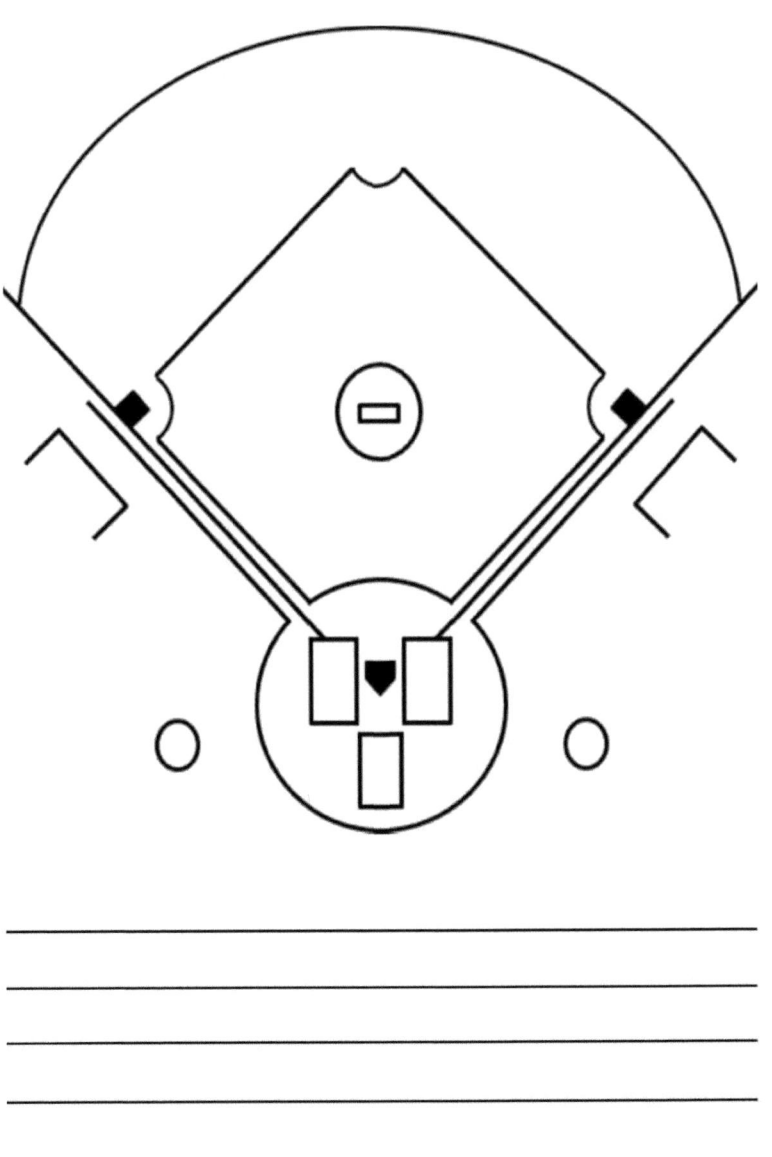

Inning of game	Player at bat	Batting position	Player number	Batter Lineup	Field position

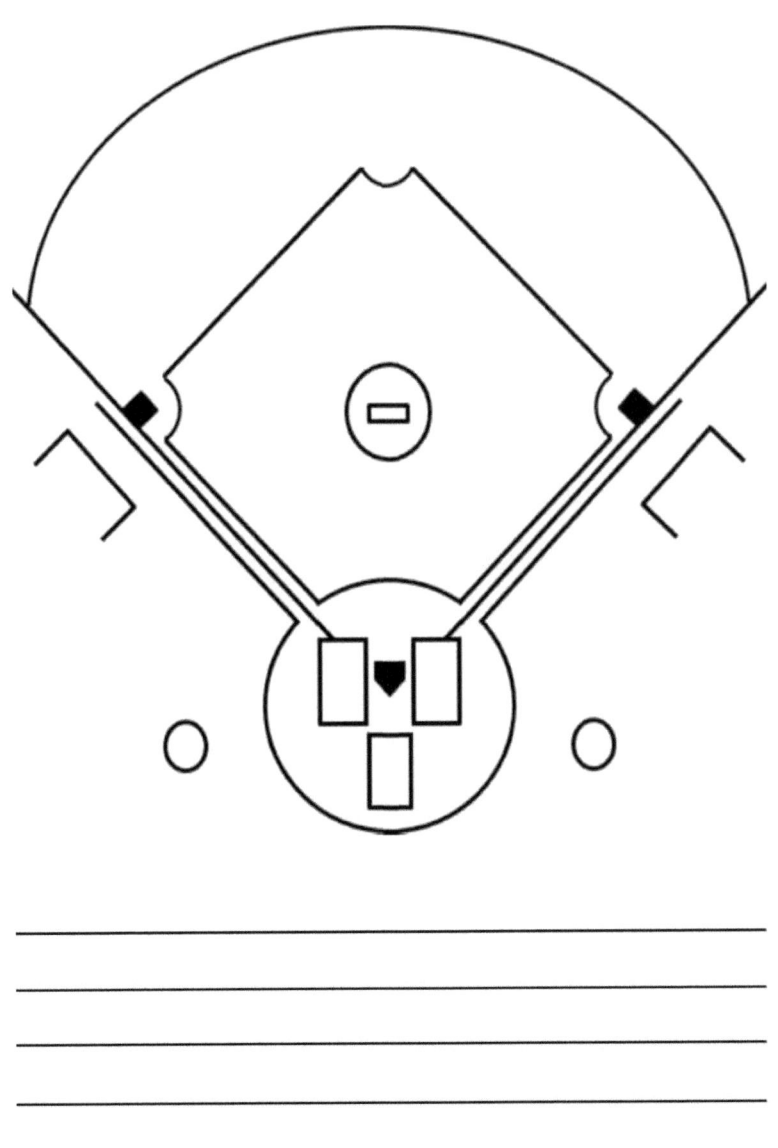

Inning of game	Player at bat	Batting position	Player number	Batter Lineup	Field position

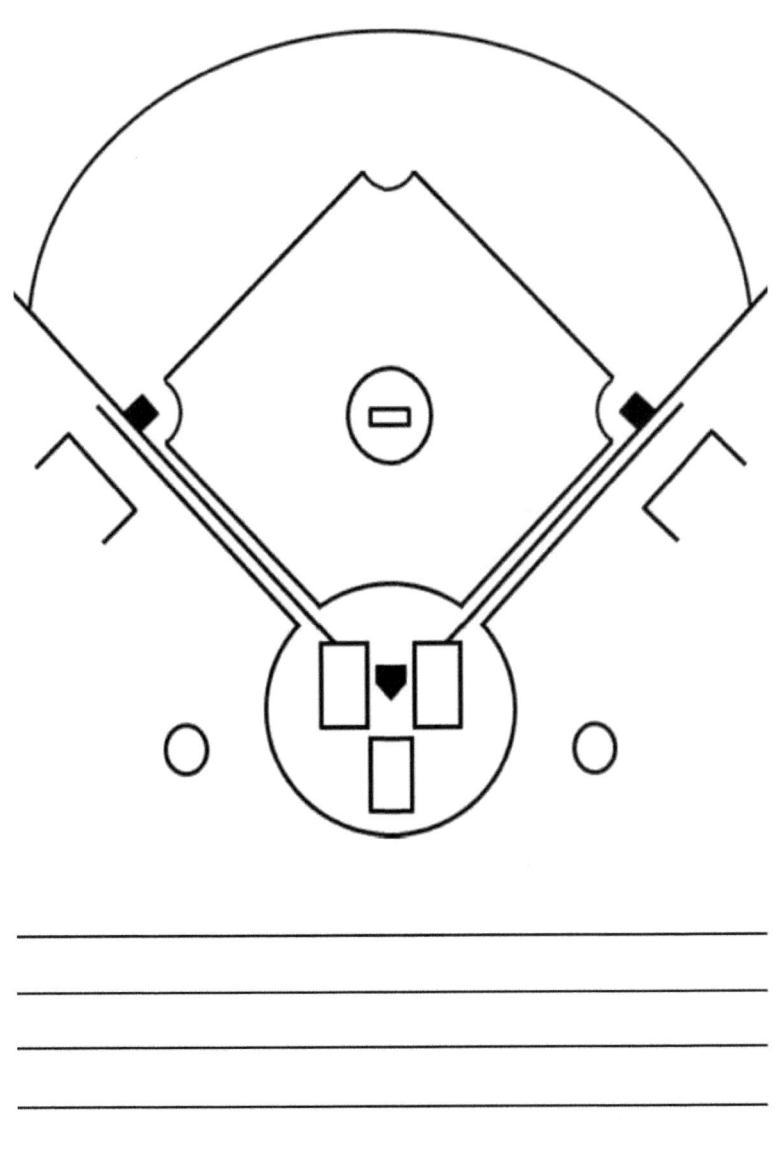

Inning of game	Player at bat	Batting position	Player number	Batter Lineup	Field position

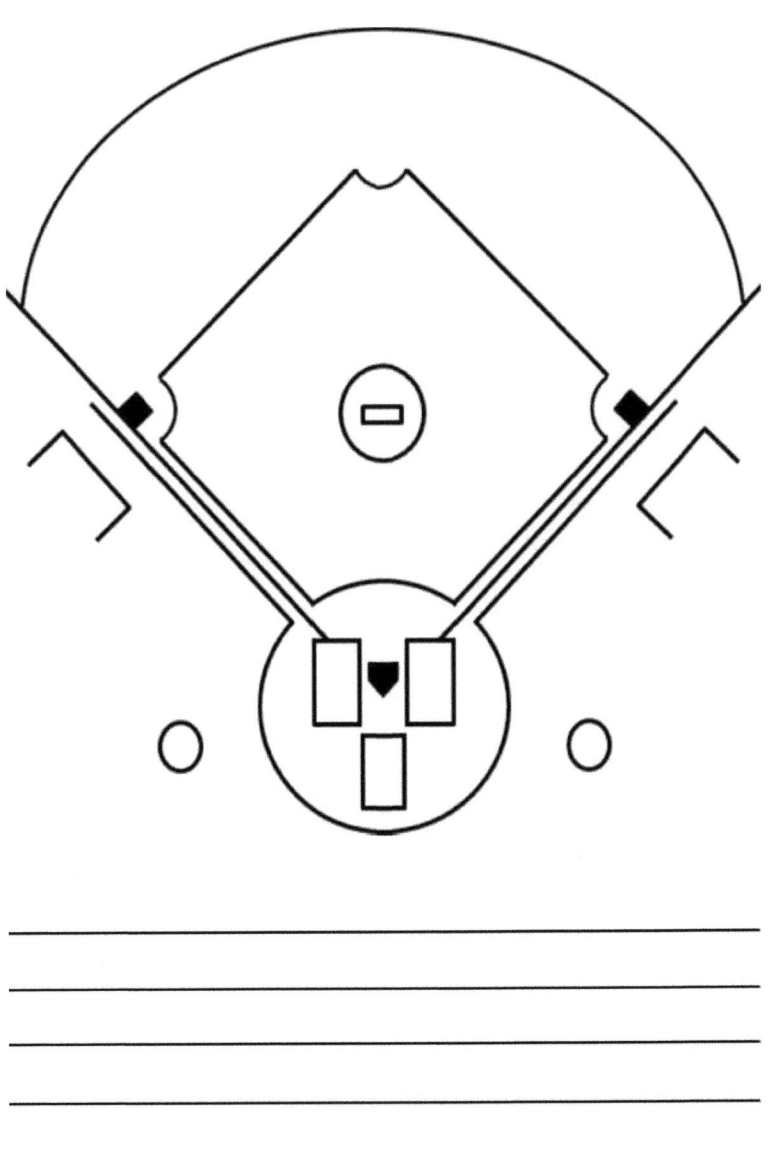

Inning of game	Player at bat	Batting position	Player number	Batter Lineup	Field position

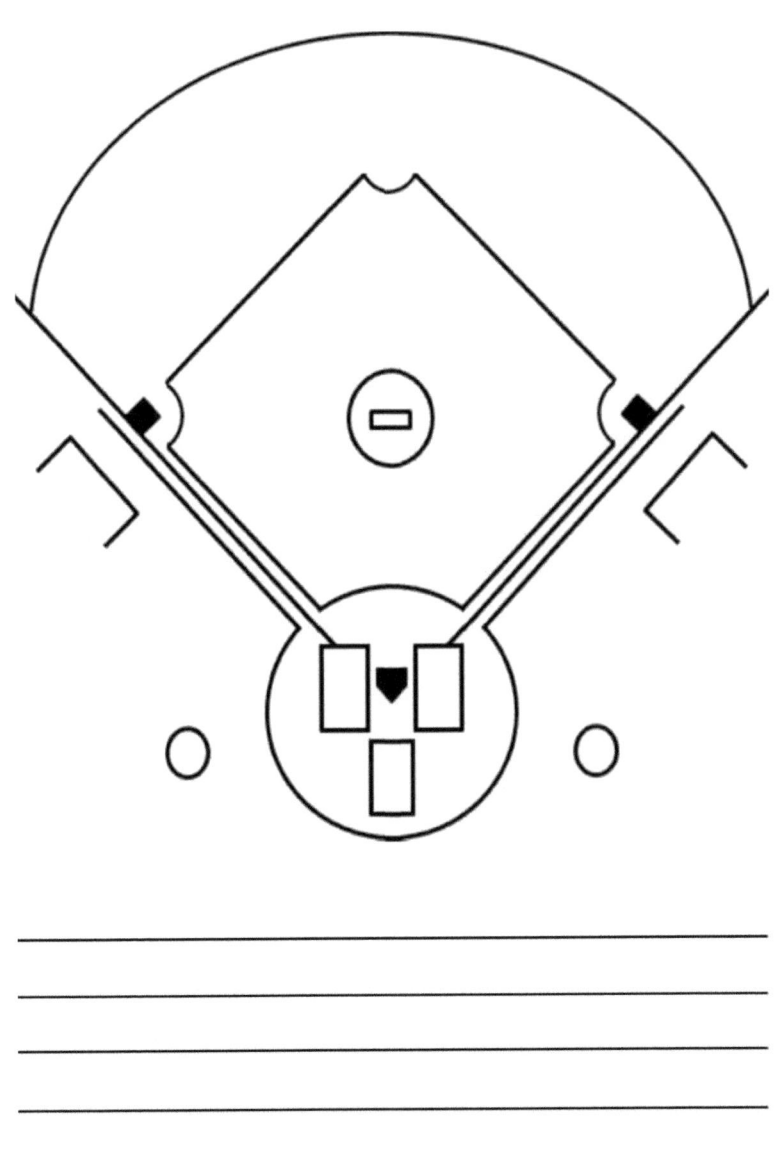

Inning of game	Player at bat	Batting position	Player number	Batter Lineup	Field position

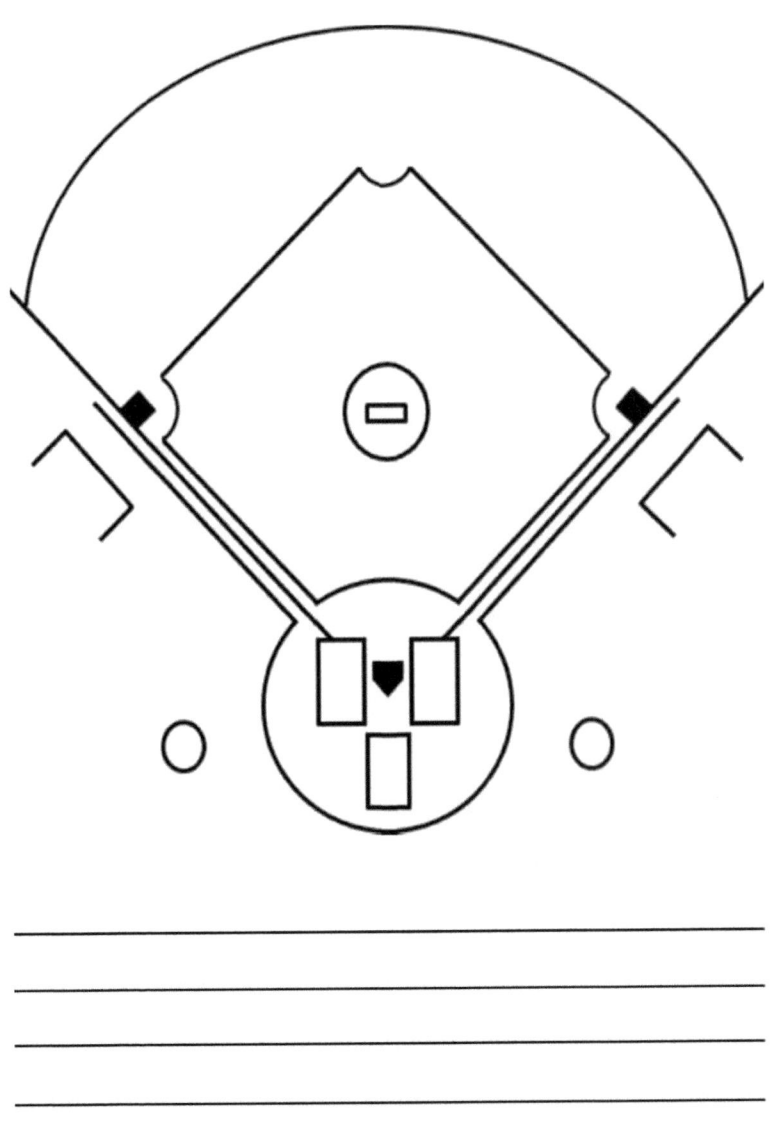

Inning of game	Player at bat	Batting position	Player number	Batter Lineup	Field position

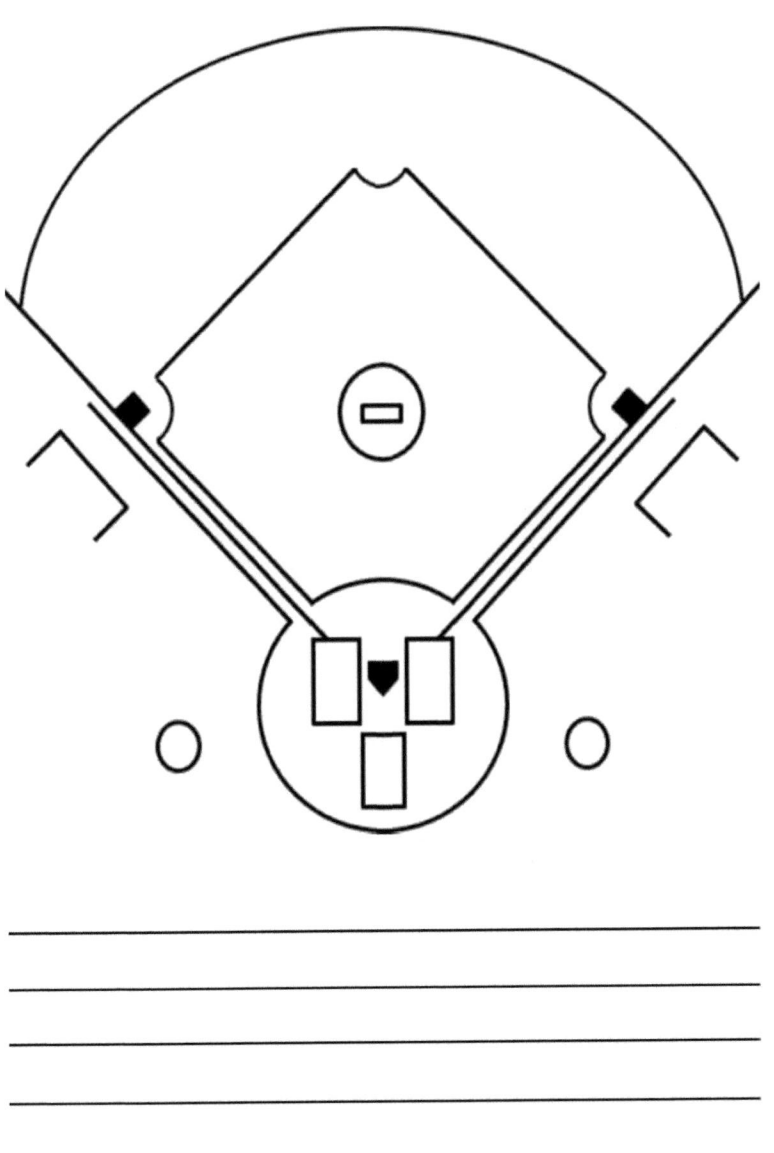

Inning of game	Player at bat	Batting position	Player number	Batter Lineup	Field position

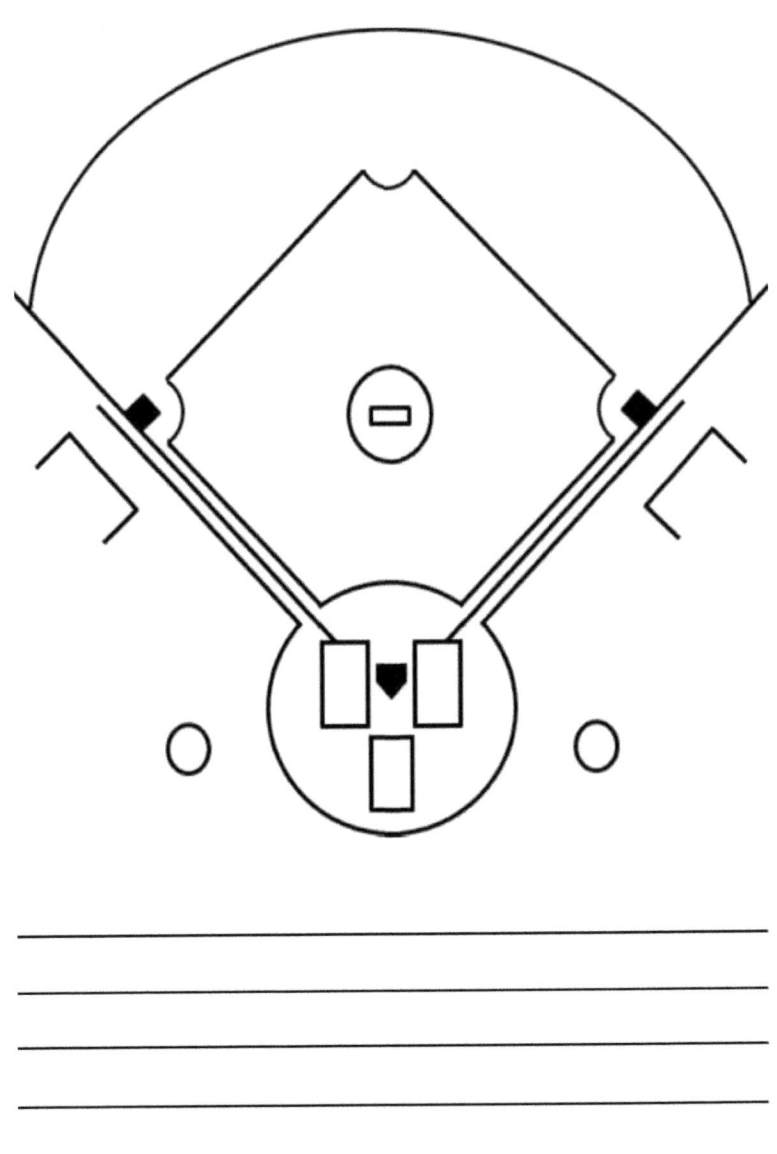

Inning of game	Player at bat	Batting position	Player number	Batter Lineup	Field position

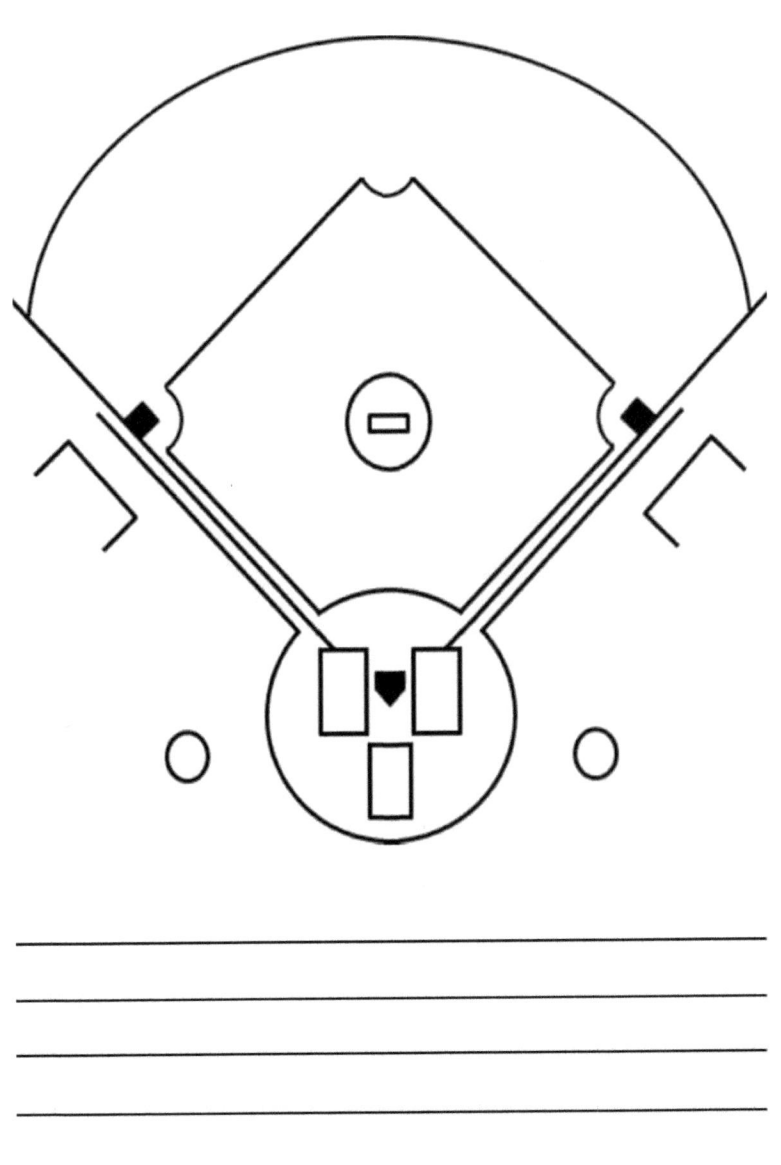

Inning of game	Player at bat	Batting position	Player number	Batter Lineup	Field position

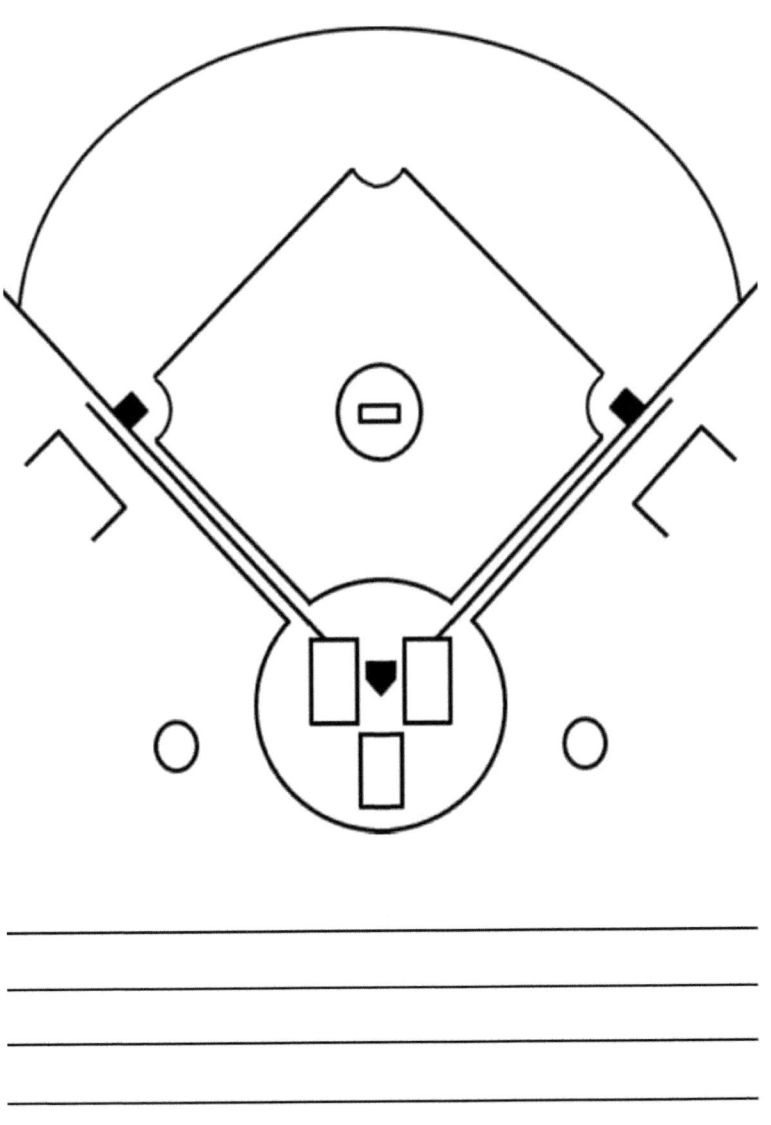

Weitere Bücher von Theo von Taane

- Happy – Wünsch dir was! — ISBN: 9783734728570
- Tennis Witze Knallbonbons — ISBN: 9783732296490
- Tennis Postkarten Kalender — ISBN: 9783734741289
- Witze rund um Volleyball — ISBN: 9783734731801
- Witze rund um Basketball — ISBN: 9783734703824
- Witze rund ums Schwimmen — ISBN: 9783734734460
- Witze rund um Schach — ISBN: 9783734731658
- Witze rund um Tischtennis — ISBN: 9783734731648
- Witze rund um Eishockey — ISBN: 9783734730716
- Witze rund ums Fechten — ISBN: 9783734731976
- Witze rund um Handball — ISBN: 9783734731690
- Witze rund um Badminton — ISBN: 9783734732875
- Witze rund um Karate — ISBN: 9783734731666
- Witze rund um Judo — ISBN: 9783734731674
- Witze rund um Golf — ISBN: 9783734731704
- Witze rund um Fußball — ISBN: 9783734731712

u.s.w.

Von Theo von Taane gibt es auch viele Rätsel-, Witze-, Spiele-, Ausmal- und Notizbüc Bücher zum Thema MINECRAFT.

Des Weiteren bietet Theo von Taane Taktikboard und Trainingsbücher auch zu folgen Sportarten an:

- Badminton
- Baseball
- Basketball
- Bowling
- Cricket
- Eishockey
- Fechten
- Feldhockey
- Fußball
- Futsal
- Handball
- Lacrosse (w)
- Lacrosse (m)
- Netball
- Rugby
- Schach
- Squash
- Tennis
- Tischtennis
- Volleyball
- Wasserball

u.v.m.
Einfach nach ‚von Taane' im Webshop suchen um sich die mehr als 200 Theo von Taane Bücher anzeigen zu lassen.